MY DOG HATES THE VET!

MY DOG HATES THE VET!
FOILING FEAR BEFORE, DURING & AFTER VET VISITS

BY

AMY SHOJAI, CABC

A QUICK TIPS GUIDE, VOL. 4

FURRY MUSE

Furry Muse Publishing
Sherman TX 75091-1904

© 2017 Amy D. Shojai

ISBN-10: 1-944423-81-8
ISBN-13: 978-1-944423-81-0

PUBLISHER'S NOTE

Every effort has been made to ensure that the information contained in this book is complete and accurate. However, neither the publisher nor the author is engaged in rendering professional advice or services to the individual reader. Further, veterinary medicine and animal behavior science continually evolve. The ideas, procedures, and suggestions contained in this book are not intended as a substitute for consulting with your pet's physician. All matters regarding your pet's health require medical supervision. Neither the author nor the publisher shall be liable or responsible for any loss or damage allegedly arising from any information or suggestion in this book.

The scanning, uploading and distribution of this book via the Internet or via any other means without the permission of the publisher is illegal and punishable by law. Please purchase only authorized electronic editions, and do not participate in or encourage electronic piracy of copyrighted materials. Your support of the author's rights is appreciated.

Publisher: Furry Muse Publishing
               PO Box 1904
               Sherman TX 75091-1904

Table of Contents

MY DOG HATES THE VET! 11
    7 Reasons Dogs Hate Vets 13
    Fearful Fido? 16

FOILING FEAR: BEFORE THE VET VISIT 19
    19 Ways To Soothe Fear Aggression 19
    Benefits Of Crates & Carriers 27
    How To Choose The Best Crate 29
    8 Tips To Crate Train Pets 31

WHY DOGS HATE CARS 35
    7 Tips For Dog Car Travel 36
    5 Ways to Soothe Canine Car Sickness 39

FOILING FEAR: DURING THE VET VISIT 42
    Picking The Best Veterinarian 42
    What To Look For In A Vet Clinic 46
    A Partnership For Dog Health 48

FOILING FEAR: AFTER THE VET VISIT 50
    Scent Communication Rules 51
    Stop After-Vet-Visit Dog Bashing 52

THANK YOU FOR READING! 55

BIO: Amy Shojai, CABC 57

DEAR DOG LOVER,

After writing 35+ pet behavior, vet care and training books, preserving "the bond" remains paws-down the most important goal of my career.

Preserving the pet-owner bond is why I wrote my quick-tips guide series. The dog behavior advice is easy to do, and will help your "pet love" grow as your family grows.

You can find lots more free dog-centric advice by subscribing to my Bling, Bitches & Blood Blog at https://amyshojai.com. You can also subscribe to the free Pets Peeves newsletter and my ASK AMY YouTube. Stay tuned for some upcoming pet-tastic care and behavior webinars! Find my books at https://Shojai.com.

I love hearing what kind of furry info-tainment readers love best—yes, I do answer email! Please write me at amy@shojai.com. Or find me on Twitter (@amyshojai) as well as on Facebook. And now—read on for paw-some step by step tips and more to help relieve your doggy's vet visit angst.

Woofs & wags,

MY DOG HATES THE VET!

My first dog Fafnir hated visiting the veterinarian. Sadly, he's no longer with us, but his angst made the last years of his life a challenge when he really NEEDED to be seen more frequently. Our current German Shepherd, Magical-Dawg, feels more welcoming of our new veterinarian's attention, but still isn't particularly eager to visit.

That's not necessarily the veterinarian's fault. Many dogs are home-bodies and love the status quo and turn into furry maniacs at the first sniff of change. Even a gregarious, never-met-a-stranger canine may become a bit shy when outside the comfort zone of his familiar home.

Of course, all dogs need veterinary checkups on a routine basis. Magic's 11th birthday was July 2017, and for these golden oldie canines, it's even more important they receive regular health checks.

Whatever your dog's age, proper veterinary care is vital to his or her wellbeing. Yet many pet parents delay or avoid taking their beloved dogs to the vet for even routine care, because, frankly, they hate putting the dog through the fear, anxiety and stress.

Maybe your dogs disappear when the carriers come out, wail and howl throughout the car ride, or turn into devil-creatures when handled by strangers. Believe me, your dogs don't want to bite you or the veterinary staff. But when they're scared, all bets are off. Nobody can think straight when in terror mode.

And oh, the embarrassment for YOU! Does the veterinary staff wince and prepare for the worst when you bring "BAD DOG" into the clinic? Is your pet's file marked with red warning notes? That's a common occurrence—but again, the times are a-changing, so read on.

BUT REX DOESN'T ACT SICK…

Dogs may hide some illness incredibly well. And maybe, like me, you hate the whining/crying complaints my first dog muttered while traveling to the vet.

Set aside for a moment the angst that you and the veterinary staff feel. Your dog's stress levels are even more important. Stress can aggravate or predispose to some kinds of health issues, make sick dogs sicker, and delay healing in recovering dogs. Stress can even falsify health test results.

Pets Deserve Fear Free Care

In the two decades since Fafnir's fear-filled clinic visits, veterinary medicine has made great strides. Today, new programs help veterinarians learn new ways to handle and treat dogs to make the experience less scary.

That reduces the "dread factor" for your dog, and you. And in turn, fear free gets Rex more timely health care. What a waggingly sensible approach!

Reducing and eliminating fear, anxiety and stress at home, on the trip to the clinic, and while at the veterinary hospital can be accomplished by providing dog-centric facilities, handling, and preparation. That means that pet parents need to offer a "paw" to help their dogs before, during and after the visit.

That's win-win for you, the vet staff, and most of all, for your dog. To do that, let's take a look at why dogs hate the vet. Only then can we take steps to address the challenges facing our dogs, and us as their caretakers.

7 Reasons Dogs Hate Vets

Crate Expectations. Dogs learn very quickly to recognize cause-and-effect. The appearance of the pet carrier prompts canine disappearing acts if they only experience the crate for trips to the vet.

Car Rides. While humans see out windows and know what's happening, the dogs-eye-view from the carrier or back seat offers movement without warning. Odd sounds and being in a strange environment raises dog blood pressure and might even prompt motion sickness. When car rides only take your buddy to the vet hospital, boarding clinic ("Don't leave me!") or groomer where they have scary experiences, the car becomes a torture chamber.

Scary Smells. Dogs experience life through their nose. The unfamiliar scent of the hospital—antiseptic, strangers, other animals—can ramp up doggy fright factor. Then when your dog returns home, the odd clinic smells cling to his fur and can make it hard for pet buddies—especially cats—to welcome him home.

Strange Pets. Nothing turns some dogs into panicked pooches like other frightened dogs and cats. When confined inside the carrier or on a leash, your scared pooch can't flee, so the fight-or-flight instinct leaves few options. She may redirect her fear aggression on the nearest target—you, or the vet staff.

Cold Table. While small dogs may hate getting into the carrier, being dumped on a cold, slick metal table elevates the "scary-strangeness" of the experience. After all, Rex's preferred lounging spots are the sofa, your bed, the floor, or your lap. High perches with slippery footing ramp up the fear.

Slick Floors. Old dogs especially have trouble keeping their feet on the shiny-clean floors of many veterinary hospitals. How do you feel during cold weather trying to navigate the walk from ice covered parking lot to the office? Some fearful dogs object to the shine, too.

Weird People. The vet and clinic staff love animals, but to your dog, strangers are from Mars. Maybe they wear uniforms like that scary UPS guy, or (gasp!) masks. Even worse, they don't ask permission to pet. The dog might be handled by several different strangers who stink of other pets' fear—the vet tech for temperature or stool sample, for example, and later the veterinarian.

Rude Handling. Having a cold thermometer inserted into doggy nether regions is no way to make friends. Needle sticks for vaccinations or blood draws for heartworm checks aren't much fun, either, but are necessary. The veterinarian and staff often must hurry the exam along, but scared dogs want and need to be romanced and wooed to gift us with their affection.

Dogs remember discomfort, fear, and bad experiences from a veterinary visit and anticipate they'll happen again in the future. But dogs also remember GOOD experiences and their expectations adjust accordingly. Don't you want your dog to be the one racing with tail wags and cries of happiness to meet the clinic staff? It's up to us to create positive experiences before, during and after the veterinary visit.

You can do this! Read on to learn more about foiling canine fear, creating positive crate expectations, and turning vet visits into wag-fests. I promise, your dogs will thank you.

Fearful Fido?
The Truth Behind Bashful Dogs

Doggy ancestors needed to be cautious, but if taken to extremes, anxiety can result in fear aggression that endangers you and the rest of your family. Extreme fear can interfere with learning, although fearful dogs still learn effective lessons about escape behavior or aggression when these behaviors make the scary situation that caused their fear to go away.

Humans can inherit a tendency to be anxious, and so can dogs. Studies indicate that up to 20 percent of any population of a given species will be born prone to introversion and fear, conditions which are worsened by abuse or lack of proper socialization.

Environment, life experience and breed tendencies also play a role. These experiences short-circuit the confidence-building puppies need so they become anxiety-ridden adults. Pain or illness that makes the dog hurt or just feel crummy also can cause anxiety. Such dogs begin to associate certain kinds of handling with discomfort, and react with fear.

Extreme fear prompted by a sound, smell, or sight can cause a panic attack, in which the dog loses his mind. One study showed that 87 percent of thunderstorm-fearful dogs also suffered from separation anxiety, and some behaviorists estimate up to 20 percent of dogs suffer from noise phobias, especially to thunder and fireworks, which can cause panic attack. These same dogs may be predisposed to vet visit fears.

Even normally friendly pets become dangerous when they are terrified. They try to get away, even going through glass windows or over people and dogs, but will get over the fear in 10 to 20 minutes. Until the panic goes away, talking or touching him can make the panic continue, so stay out of his way and let Rex hide and calm down.

Fearfulness prompts increased heart and breathing rate, and scared dogs signal unease with yawns, pinning ears back, tucking tail, urinating or even defecating. Signs of anxiety include staring, panting, shaking, crouching, squinting, furrowed brow, and whale eye.

Besides being unhealthy, nervous and fearful dogs aren't happy pets, or fun to be around, and, above all, we want our dogs to enjoy life. Some types of fear will never go away, but usually can be helped so the dog feels better most of the time.

Any change of routine can threaten a dog's sense of security. Timid and shy dogs react with fear to unfamiliar people, places or situations, because they assume the worst. A vet visit delivers a triple-whammy by changing the dog's routine, environment, and exposure to strangers.

A strange environment like the vet clinic or the car turns up canine nerves because the boogyman might lurk in some unknown spot. Scary sounds, sights and smells make fearful dogs even more scared. Your dog won't know the escape routes or safety zones, so fear becomes the default emotion. Frightened dogs either freeze, or defend themselves. In fact, dogs that default to "freeze" at the vet hospital might appear to tolerate exams and stranger handling, but all the while they actually feel terrified. Poor dogs!

While a normal dose of caution keeps dogs from becoming coyote kibble, constant anxiety increases stress that can make dogs sick. For instance, stress can aggravate digestive upset, which in turn prompts hit-or-miss bathroom behaviors. Skin disease and allergies often are aggravated by stress. The lick-lick-licking and chewing behavior can be turned into a comforting ritual dogs use to cope with anxiety.

Scared dogs quickly learn that aggressive behavior makes the scary "thing" go away. They use it repeatedly to warn off strangers, for example, with growls and snarls of warning.

Aggression that arises from fear can make pet parents reluctant to take dogs to the clinic for important veterinary care. And it can make the veterinary staff reluctant to handle your dog, too. By recognizing the signs of fear aggression, and following a few tips, you can help your dog feel less frightened and more confident. That makes it easy for the vet staff to agree just how special Rex really is.

FOILING FEAR:

BEFORE THE VET VISIT

Helping Rex become more tolerant won't happen overnight. Begin during puppyhood for the best result. But many adult dogs also show an incredible positive change in attitude simply by following these tips.

19 Ways To Soothe Fear Aggression

If the dog's fear aggression is mild and you can avoid the triggers that make Rex aggress, no other treatment may be necessary. These tips can help diffuse the fear, and you can use these at home. So can your vet, in the clinic itself.

Socialize Puppies. Dogs learn how to be dogs very early, as puppies. The people and experiences that babies first encounter teaches both positive and negative lessons that follow Rex the rest of his life. Think of yourself and the vet staff as kindly uncles, guiding the inexperienced youngsters' development. That's a huge responsibility! Socialization refers to how baby dogs learn to interact with the world around them—you, other dogs and animals, and other people. Canine learning involves both nature (genetics) and nurture (environment). Puppies that inherit the potential for aggression and shyness, for example, may never exhibit these problems if properly socialized.

The prime socialization period for puppies ranges from about six to twelve weeks of age, tapering on up to sixteen weeks of age, but socialization continues after this. It's an ongoing process—you won't be "done" once you reach a particular date. Rex will need refreshers throughout his life, especially if he has a tendency toward shyness. When you first adopt your puppy, expose the youngster to happy, positive experiences with a variety of strangers, locations and other pets. That helps him learn that other people, places, and critters can be fun and not scary. For example, take your puppy to visit and be handled by the staff at the veterinary clinic so his only experience isn't a scary needle stick.

Determine Distance Issues. Most normal dogs tolerate one dog length and a half (their own length) before feeling uncomfortable. A fearful dog's sensitive distance may be much greater, and if another dog or person approaches within that range he attacks. Avoid situations by maintaining an appropriate distance between the fearful dog and potential triggers. In the vet clinic situation, that can mean moving holding cages further apart, for example, to keep strange animals a safer distance away.

Cage aggression occurs when a dog can't back away from your reaching hands when the cage or crate door opens, and he defends the space with snarls and teeth. Avoid cage aggression by opening the door and backing away, using a food lure to tempt the dog to exit on his own. At the clinic, veterinarians and staff can help prevent this type of reaction by examining dogs in open spaces where they don't feel trapped. Many bites take place in tight doorways and entrance/exits where dogs have little room to escape.

Speak With Confidence. Speak to your shy dog in a calm, happy tone as if he's already well adjusted. Dogs may not understand all the words, but will recognize if you're happy with them, aggravated, amused, or affectionate. The more you speak to your dogs, the better they will learn to understand and react to what you want. That enhances and improves your relationship. Avoid yelling which can prompt submissive urination. Certainly you can comfort your scared dog, but that alone won't change the behavior, and you want to encourage confidence. Try instead to ignore any shivering and praise for outgoing, confident behaviors. Watch for relaxed breathing, calm expressions and body postures.

Say Howdy. Teach your dog the phrase 'say howdy' that signals to Rex the person is safe to meet. You also can teach "look" while pointing at various places and objects to tell your dog it's safe to investigate. Once dogs know these phrases, you can use them at the clinic to meet the veterinarian and staff. At home, increase healthy curiosity and confidence by hiding tasty treats underneath a towel or cushion, toy or other object so when the dog investigates, there's a reward waiting.

Sit Down. Standing over top of small dogs intimidates them, but squatting can also seem scary. Facing directly toward a dog also may seem intimidating. When a dog is shy of people, sit on the floor some distance away, turned sideways, and let the dog come to you.

Pet The Chest. Fearful dogs can be hand shy so avoid petting doggy heads. Hands coming down from above can be scary, especially from strangers, and increase anxiety. Reaching for the scared dog's collar almost always precipitates a bite. Instead pet the dog's chest or neck but only if he's willing.

Don't Stare. To the dog, direct eye contact can be a threat. Instead, ignore the dog—no eye contact at all. Let the dog approach and control the interaction.

Provide Enrichment. At home, create a house of plenty by providing lots of toys, chew objects, beds and feeding stations to reduce competition with other pets. Offer dog viewing fun by setting up bird baths and squirrel feeders outside windows. Some dogs enjoy wildlife videos, and the vet clinic might employ a doggy TV to help distract your shy dog during the exam.

Let Him Walk. People often feel protective of lap-sized breeds, and carry them everywhere. This will encourage shyness and tells tiny dogs the danger is real. Allow small dogs to keep four paws on the ground, and they'll be more confident as a result.

Use A Floor Matt. If you know your dog has slick floor issues, invest in a take-along floor covering like a yoga mat. That way, Rex can practice walking, sitting and even sleeping on his own personal Rex-scented matt in the comfort of his own home. And you can take it with you for him to strut his mutt-stuff once at the clinic. Some vet clinics now stock yoga mats for this purpose, and spritz them with a pheromone-type product that also helps ease the angst.

Give Them Calming Sniff. Use of dog pheromone products both at home and in clinic situations ease stress in the dog's territory and/or relationships. Today, these products come as sprays, impregnated collars, and plug-in diffusers.

Provide Soothing Sounds. Music therapy works incredibly well to calm doggy stress. New age sounds, classical music, and tempos that mimic a resting heartbeat help enormously. Harp music is a natural sedative for which you need no prescription. Some music today has been designed specifically with dogs in mind.

Offer Natural Help. Treats with natural ingredients like valerian or melatonin are designed to help calm dogs, and some may work quite well when given prior to a scary event. Calming hoods and caps that cover the eyes or muffle sounds, as well as swaddling and pressure type garments also help some dogs. Pressure garments can be worn to the vet clinic, too, and may take the edge off the anxiety. Rescue Remedy or similar products can also help shy and fearful pets. We're not sure how these vibrational therapies really work. Some professionals suspect the placebo effect influences effectiveness but—if it reduces Rex's stress, I'm all for placebo effect!

Create Routines. Shy and fearful dogs become more fearful if given choices, so provide lots of direction and create a schedule so your dog knows when to expect meals, a walk, potty breaks, and everything else. Routine builds security that allows shy dogs to become more relaxed. Once he recognizes you are in charge and he doesn't need to be responsible, some of the fear may go away. When you've established a routine—perhaps a particular obedience command always results in a treat—your veterinarian can incorporate that in the exam routine, too.

Use Play Therapy. Interactive play builds canine confidence. A favorite game or toy can be a familiar comfort, and normalize the clinic visit, even when in the hands of the veterinary nurse during the visit. When dogs engage in fun games, their brains can't be happy and scared at the same time. Take a cue from cat toys—terriers and small dogs especially may like these—and use a long distance interactive fishing-pole lure toy. That can teach shy dogs that you (or the veterinarian) are fun to be around, but without having to get too close. That can lure the anxious dog close, so you avoid scaring him with grabby hands that may reinforce his fear of strangers handling him. A game of catch the squeaky to reward bravery can do wonders for the shy dog's attitude.

Offer Treats. If your dog loves food, offer smelly treats to diffuse the angst. Have the vet staff drop or toss treats when they arrive at the exam room door, so their entry signals "food" instead of "stranger danger." Aerosol cheese and liverwurst can really get the tails wagging. Chow hounds often forget they're scared as long as they're lapping up the goodies.

Give Smell-Rewards. Some dogs, especially hunting breeds, may prefer a pungent sniff rather than an edible treat. For these dogs, create a stinky-sock reward to distract them. Fill a sock with a very aromatic distinctive smell, perhaps something like dehydrated salmon. Or even (yuck!) a critter lure available from hunting supply stores like coyote urine or fox musk. Keep this in a sealable plastic bag, and offer a sniff to the dog to keep his attention focused on you and not what the veterinary procedure might entail.

Pet With Intent. Pleasant touch prompts a reduction in blood pressure and heart rate, and can change brain wave activity. Studies have shown that handling furry babies for five minutes a day during their first three weeks increases the pet's ability to learn later in life. So from the beginning, partner tasty treats with touch and pleasant handling that mimics what the veterinary staff will do during exams and treatment. Handle your dog's paws, for example, then give a schmear of Philly cream cheese. Look in Cinder's ears and rub that itchy spot she can't reach, while you praise and offer a taste of peanut butter. Have another family member hold a frozen pupsicle treat (chicken broth in a Kong works well!), while you pet Rex from head to tail, or even (GASP!) clip a claw or two. Make these touches a part of your dogs' routine so they recognize this when they visit the vet. Veterinary staff can use the same techniques of offering aerosol cheese to distract the dog while a second technician gives a vaccination.

Teach A Default Behavior. Training builds confidence and helps improve the bond you share. You can use clicker training to communicate with your dog, and associate positive things (treats, toys, attention) with otherwise angst-causing situations like vet visits, car rides or crate training. Teach the fearful dog a specific command for a contradictory behavior that helps him avoid the scary trigger, and/or changes his emotional state. For instance, "go-to-bed" command can be taught as a default behavior when the doorbell rings, so the dog is in a safe happy place far from where strangers enter the house. Or a "where's your ball?" cue can change the fear to fun, and dogs can learn to find this security-item when feeling stressed. Take the security item with you during vet visits, so Rex has something to do when he feels angsty.

CANINE CRATE TRAINING

Why would you want to "cage" your dog and put him in puppy jail? The way some dogs howl and complain, you'd think the incarceration is torture. Isn't confinement mean?

Actually, it's not. Most puppies and adult dogs feel more secure in a small, enclosed den-like area. That's not to say your dog should be in the crate for outrageous lengths of time. A youngster should be introduced slowly to the crate when possible and not left unattended longer than he's able to "hold it" for potty training.

Benefits Of Crates & Carriers

Most dogs feel more secure in a small, enclosed den-like area, especially when they feel anxious. So using a carrier for trips to the vet can actually ease the angst, once your dog has been properly acclimated to it. The dog's personal familiar carrier or crate may be left with the vet should an extended stay be necessary. It's easiest to introduce puppies to the concept but dogs of any age can be taught that a carrier/crate is a very-good-dog-spot.

Prime Nap Spot. A crate works well as a bed. When a pet claims the spot for naps, it's no longer scary, but becomes a happy, familiar place he feels secure.

Private Retreat. Because it's enclosed, a crate also serves as a safe retreat to get away from other pets or pestering children. Don't you want a private place of your own where you won't be bothered? Dog are no different.

Safe Confinement. Some carriers undergo safety crash tests for extra peace of mind during travel. A crate also can be the safest place to confine your precious dog to keep him from pottying in the wrong spot, chewing up the furniture or doorway dashing when you can't watch him. Once he learns that his crate is a wonderful doggy benefit, it can be a comfort to dogs when they travel by car or stay at the veterinarian, for example.

How To Choose The Best Crate

The perfect crate or carrier should be just large enough for a pet to go inside, turn around, and lie down to sleep. It can be a solid hard plastic container, wire mesh cage or soft-sided duffle style. Of course, puppies grow, so take into account your dog's future adult size before investing in a pricy crate.

Large crates are available with partitions for you to "shrink" to puppy size, and then enlarge the area as your puppy grows. You can also purchase an adult-size crate, and insert a barrier like a plastic storage box that shrinks the space to puppy proportions until your pet grows into the size. While soft-sided pet carriers work great for transporting small to medium size dogs, they may be too small for larger pets or prove too tempting for chew-aholic dogs to work well for safe confinement.

Put yourself in your dog's "paws" to help choose the best carrier. How would you feel about having a stranger's huge hands (as big as your whole body!) reach into your personal space, grab and drag you out of a cozy bed? Associating the carrier with that scary experience means the dog hides the next time it makes an appearance.

The best crates and carriers for small dogs have a couple of openings for the dog to go in and out without being forced. Look for those that have both a side and a top easy access opening. Instead of forcing him into or dragging him out of the carrier, you can simply lift away part of the enclosure. The vet may be able to perform an exam while the dog never leaves the comfort of his bed.

Some of the hard-sided crates come apart so that the top simply lifts off the pet. There are also round carriers which zipper open and close like a clam shell, making access to the dog a breeze and far less angst-inspiring. That's important whether your dogs are fearful, or illness and mobility makes them reluctant to move.

8 Tips To Crate Train Pets

The key to training dogs to accept the carrier is to create familiarity. You do that by introducing him to this new situation in a series of non-threatening, gradual steps.

If your dog is already fearful of the crate, getting a new one without those old, scary associations may help. Also, ask your veterinarian about medication that may help reduce anxiety or nausea. Some dog hate going to the vet because they get car sick, and scared dogs can't learn new things when they are fearful.

Introduced correctly, your dog will welcome and even enjoy spending time in his crate. The crate should never be a place of punishment if you want him to consider it a pleasant experience. So use these tips to help your dog claim the space as his own home-sweet-home.

Location Is Key. While well-adjusted dogs often are curious, some tend toward shyness. Anything new prompts suspicion. So make the crate or carrier "part of the furniture" and set it out in a safe, familiar place like your bedroom or the family room for your dog to explore. It should be convenient for you to access, too, and away from lots of traffic so the dog has a private place to retreat. Leave the carrier open so he can sniff it inside and out. Take a cue from your dog's current favorite hangouts, and offer a location he already loves. Don't make a big deal out of it. Once your puppy accepts the crate as a fact of puppy life, you can move the crate to a more acceptable spot in the house. A place next to your own bed will let the dog sleep in his own spot but near your familiar smells and presence. That also offers you a more private area to seclude him, when necessary, from activities in the living area or kitchen that might keep him over stimulated.

Make It A Happy Place. Place a snuggly blanket inside, or even a fuzzy shirt that YOU have worn. That associates the carrier with your familiar and trusted scent. Adding a spritz of a canine "no-fear" pheromone product like D.A.P. with Comfort Zone also may help. You'll have that same fuzzy scented blanket to spread on the examining table or floor at the vet clinic, too, so your dog isn't shocked by the weird smelling surroundings.

Add A Toy or Game. Toss a squeaky toy inside to create positive experiences with the crate. Tennis balls are great fun inside the hard crates. Reserve his favorite toy or game to use only near or inside the carrier to elevate the benefit of hanging out in the carrier.

Offer A Treat. Find a puzzle toy that can be stuffed with a smelly, tasty treat. This should be a treat your dog loves, but he ONLY gets the treat when inside the crate. Show it to him, and let him smell and taste the treat. Then toss it inside the crate and shut the door—with the dog OUTSIDE the crate and the treat on the inside. Some puzzle toys can be attached to the inside of the crate door, making it even more enticing. That shows him that an absolutely scrumptious treat is inside, out of paw-reach. Only after he's begged and scratched and whined to get inside should you open the door and let him get the toy. Allow him to chew and enjoy it for five minutes with the door shut. If he wants out, let him out—but the treat stays inside. This exercise teaches him to make the choice to tolerate staying confined, with a bonus reward for putting up with the confinement.

Teach Him Tolerance. After your dog spends time willingly inside, increase the episodes of crate time. Most dogs tolerate the door shut at least as long as they have something to munch. Praise the dickens out of him! He should know that staying calmly inside the crate earns him good things. Repeat several times over the next few days.

Extend Crate Time. By the end of the week, you can begin increasing the time the dog spends in the crate. Some dogs feel calmer when inside the carrier if you cover it with a towel because this shuts out at least the visual cues that may raise stress. Scent the towel with the D.A.P. with Comfort Zone.

Carry Him Around. Once your dog feels comfortable in the carrier with the door shut, drop in a couple of treats and then pick up the carrier while he's in it and carry him around. Give him another treat or play a favorite game as soon as you let him out.

Visit The Car. Finally, take him in the carrier out to the car, sit there and talk to him, then bring him back into the house and release him—don't forget to offer the treat. Repeat the car visit several times before you go any further.

This step-by-step plan works, but slow and steady is the name of the game. Plan on a couple of weeks (not days!) so that your dog is prepared well before ending up in the carrier at the vet. Soon, you should be able to take him for car rides in his carrier, without him throwing a fit.

WHY DOGS HATE CARS

Our dogs can't imagine something that's never happened to them before. Instead, they remember past experiences and believe the same thing will happen again. Because a pup's first car trips aren't always that pleasant, some dogs dread traveling thereafter.

The first ride in the car takes him away from the only family he's ever known. He may even get car sick during the trip. Our dog Fafnir's first car ride made him sick, and thereafter, just the thought of getting in the car made him shiver and shake—and cry and whimper the entire trip. If your dog suffers from car sickness, check out the tips in the next section.

For youngsters, when the first several rides end up at the veterinarian for scary medical treatments, it's no wonder dogs get their tails in a twist over car rides. Although you have no choice but to try and comfort your new pet, when you whine back at the shivering puppy, you've reinforced his idea that a car ride IS horrible.

Instead, help your dogs to associate cars with fun, happy experiences instead of just trips to the vet. The process, called desensitization using classical conditioning, takes patience and time, but works whether your dog acts scared, sick, or just hyper. We did this with our current dog Magic, and now he ADORES the car. I even call our car the Magic Mobile because he treats it like his own personal fun spot.

7 Tips For Dog Car Travel

Use A Restraint. For safety's sake, small to medium size dogs should ride inside a carrier while in the car. A loose pet becomes a furry projectile in case of an accident. The driver needs to concentrate on the road and traffic, not the bouncy baby on a lap or under the pedals. Even well-behaved dogs loose in the car could be injured, because an airbag will crush the crate and pet if on the front seat during an accident. So be sure to crate train the dog before you hit the road. For bigger dogs, use car barriers to keep pets in the back seat, and ideally, a halter that can be seat-belted for security.

Make Meal Time Car Time. For very frightened pups just set the bowl next to the car. After several days when she's used to that, feed her in the back seat while leaving the car door open. In between times, throw treats in the open car door for the pup to find, and play fun games near the car. She should learn that only these good things in life happen when you're near the car.

Give Smell Comfort. Place the dog's bed, blanket, or a towel you've petted her with on the back seat of the car. That way, her scent is already inside. Spraying D.A.P. with Comfort Zone on the towel or car upholstery also may help the dog feel more relaxed.

Let Her Explore. Even if she'll be inside a crate, it's helpful for dogs to experience positive things about the car before you start the engine. So once the carrier is securely in the closed car, sit beside your dog and open the carrier door. Allow her to explore if she wants, but don't force it. Next, when your pup's eating or otherwise distracted in the back seat, get in the front seat behind the steering wheel. Just sit for a while, no big deal, then get out, so she understands nothing scary happens when you're in the car too. Do this for one day.

Add the Crate or Seatbelt. You should be combining the crate training with car visits. Once the dog accepts the car, place her in the carrier, set it on the back seat (away from air bag danger), with favorite toys or treats. If she's too big for the crate, this step includes engaging the halter/leash seatbelt restraint. Once that's done, get in the front seat, and start the car. Then turn off the motor and take the dog out without going anywhere. Do this three or four times during the day until the dog takes it as a matter of course. Each time, you'll give lots of play or other rewards once she's released from the crate or seat belt. The next step adds opening the garage door (if you have one) which can be noisy and scary for some dogs. Again, repeat the process combined with treats until your dog accepts this as a normal part of her life.

Increase The Time. Finally, after you start the car, back the car to the end of the driveway and stop—do this two or three times in a row, always letting the pet out after you return. If the puppy whines or paces or shows stress, you may be moving too fast for him. Continue increasing the car-time by increments—a trip around the block and then home, then a trip to the nearest fun place like the park before returning home. Go somewhere you know your dog will enjoy—get him French fries at the nearest fast food drive through, or a doggy treat from the tellers at the bank or dry cleaner. Make every car trip upbeat and positive so the experience makes the dog look forward to the next trip.

Visit The Vet. As mentioned earlier, it's ideal for your dog to have visits to the vet that are FUN and result in playing, petting and treats, with no scary or unpleasant experiences. That prepares Rex for the times when a veterinary exam is necessary. Try to plan two to three "fun" vet visits before the actual exam.

5 Ways to Soothe Canine Car Sickness

Magical-Dawg loves car rides and has never had a problem with motion sickness. He'd drive the car if I let him. But my first dog hated the car from his very first ride home as a puppy, when he got car sick from the motion, stress and excitement. From thereafter, I believe he remembered the bad experience and dreaded the car as a result.

It's not surprising puppies may not like car rides. Puppies are not yet physically mature. Many won't have fully developed their equilibrium, and as a result often have problems with motion sickness. Often, they outgrow this as they become more mature, but they still remember the bad experience as adult dogs. New experiences can cause stress that makes it more likely puppies get car sick. And let's face it, a puppy faces something new nearly every day!

When a new experiences causes fear, pain or bad feelings like an upset tummy, the puppy can in turn associate that bad feeling with the experience—a car ride or being locked in a crate, for example. In these cases, it can turn into a vicious cycle where the memory of being sick makes him feel so bad, he gets sick and fears the experience time after time.

You can ease the upset feelings and settle his tummy with a little preparation, though. Here are some helpful ways you can reduce the chance your puppy or adult dog will get sick during his next car rides.

Relieve Stress. Puppies associate sick feelings from what they anticipate will happen at the end of the ride. To change his mind, turn the car into a puppy palace of toys and treats he only gets near – or while inside – the car. Follow the tips in the previous section to change the car association into a positive experience.

Timing Meals. If the dog has nothing in his tummy to vomit, he'll be less likely to feel sick. Treats are great for changing his car association into a happy place, but make these treats tiny—just a taste, and not a full meal. Feed him several hours BEFORE you hit the road. Be sure to offer water, though, because that can help settle an ify tummy.

Viewing Pleasures. The motion of moving cars without a view of where he's going tends to upset tummies. Tiny pups and Toy-size breeds may not be able to see out the window, though, but when he's larger and able to window gaze, that can help your dog orient himself. Just ensure he's safely restrained in a safe puppy carrier or other restraint, preferably in the back seat to avoid the danger of airbag deployment that could injure him. Also, a car barrier that keeps your dog out of your lap keeps you from becoming distracted, and also limits how much mess he can spread around the inside of your car.

Breathing Tips. Crack open the window for some fresh air for your dog's sniffing pleasure. All those fresh smells carried on the wind distract him from his ify tummy action, and a narrow opening lets him sniff without risking eye injury. You'll also want to stop and let the dog stroll around for potty breaks and sniffing-fixes during car rides, which also can help him associate positive fun things with the whole experience.

Tummy Treatments. The same drug people take to fight motion sickness works in dogs, too, and Dramamine is considered safe for most healthy adult dogs. Just be sure to check with your vet on the proper dose. Also ask about a newer option called Cerenia that's made especially for carsick dogs. You can also try offering a natural nausea remedy—ginger. You can find ginger capsules at health food stores. Dogs under 16 pounds can safely take 250-milligrams or less of ginger, while those over 16 pounds can usually handle up to 500 milligrams of ginger. Or offer the dog several ginger snap cookies. Eating cookies in the car can be a great positive association for the dog, too. Be aware that ginger cookies can stain light fur, though, if he munches and drools.

FOILING FEAR:

DURING THE VET VISIT

Picking The Best Veterinarian

People become veterinarians because they like and care about animals. Your dog deserves to be cared for by a professional that you trust. Every pet needs routine health care, and as Rex matures, some extra health care may be needed.

Veterinary medicine is in constant evolution, with advances made every day. Today, veterinarians can specialize in different areas of pet care. Most puppies receive optimum care their whole lives from general practice veterinarians. These professionals often are neighbors and become friends. In the best situations, they come to know your pets almost as well as you do.

Of course, you live with Cinder and know her best—and can tell the doctor something's wrong if she suddenly has no interest in her squeaky toy the way she normally does. This partnership means you stay alert to any warnings, then your veterinarian deals with the medical issues specific to your pets. Hopefully your pets only need to see the veterinarian a couple of times a year for general checkups and preventive care.

Some individual practices or doctors may suit your needs better than others. Your ideal veterinarian should offer:

- Office hours and location convenient to your schedule
- Fee and payment structure you can afford
- Emergency services either through their clinic or shared with other facilities
- Knowledgeable and personable staff
- Value added—some practices include boarding, grooming, or training facilities

Personality of the doctor certainly can be an issue. You should like or at least respect each other, and the doctor should care about your pets, and be willing to explain treatments and answer your questions. Conversely, you must be willing to provide necessary information, respect the doctor's time and expertise, and trust his or her judgment.

Take the time to develop a positive relationship with the people who care for your dog—and all the pets you love. After all, you're on the same team and want the same things—to create the pet of your dreams.

One of the best ways to find a veterinarian is to ask people you trust for a recommendation. When your dog is from a local breeder, a veterinarian may be available who is already familiar with the dog's relatives. Shelters often have staff veterinarians or shelter clinics that offer services to adopted pets and their owners. Don't forget to ask family and friends who they trust to care for their special pets. Savvy shelters and rescue operations today use some of the same techniques as vet clinics to ensure their facilities and staff are fear free and dog friendly.

Ask whether the veterinary practice is AAHA accredited. AAHA stands for American Animal Hospital Association, which was founded more than 80 years ago. It is a voluntary accrediting organization for small animal hospitals in the United States. Only 12-15 percent of animal hospitals have gone through the rigorous and stringent evaluation process to attain this distinction. You can do a search online to find an AAHA-accredited practice at this link: https://www.aaha.org.

Multi-veterinary practices offer a wide range of services all under one roof. You'll likely have one primary care doctor for your dog. At the same time, your pet will benefit from others within the practice who offer specialized care in specific areas. For instance, a board-certified internist offers expertise in diagnosis of certain health problems above and beyond what a general practice veterinarian may be able to provide.

One of the newest certification programs, Fear Free, is open to individuals (veterinarians, vet techs, behaviorists, trainers and other pet professionals), as well as entire practices and dog-trainer-specific courses. The guiding principle is to remove the fear-based obstacles that make vet visits an unpleasant experience for you, your pets, and the medical staff. By implementing fear free practices, dogs no longer fear vet visits, which eliminates YOUR dread about putting them through the experience. Happy, calm dogs are easier for clinic staff to provide the best care. You can learn more about Fear Free certification at this link: https://www.fearfreepets.com.

In the best of all possible worlds, you'll be able to choose a veterinarian and practice that is dog-friendly, AAHA-certified, and Fear Free. Don't be shy about asking local practitioners. Your questions may be what inspires them to go the extra paw-step to become certified!

What To Look For In A Vet Clinic

It's a good idea to make an appointment to visit a potential veterinary clinic ahead of time. The doctor's office is a busy place, though, so call to schedule a time when the staff isn't tied up with surgery or appointments. Chat with the office manager, technicians, and the veterinarian when possible, and ask for a brief tour of the facilities. Some things to consider include:

Is the clinic certified by AAHA or Fear Free? Those designations offer peace of mind, with a standard you can trust. Such practices are more likely to have separate waiting rooms for dogs and cats, because that can ease the stress level of the pets. Ideally, they also have a separate quarantine area to keep ill animals from being near healthy dogs.

Dog friendly practices may provide bubbling water drinking fountains, play pet videos and calming music, or display bird houses near examining room windows to help keep dogs calm. Rather than cold metal tables or slick floors, the exam surface and flooring may be more skid-proof, with the opportunity for floor-level dog exams for the big guys. Find out if you're allowed to stay with your dog during exams, or if furry patients are treated out of sight. And ask how the staff typically handles frightened dogs, and what types of restraints (if any) are typically used and under what circumstances.

Are boarding or grooming facilities available? If you need to go out of town or your Poodle requires fur-attention, you may feel much more comfortable leaving Cinder and Rex in the expert care of the hospital staff they know and like.

What about emergency and referral services? If the worst happens, you want to have access to life-saving care. Practices often partner with other vet clinics to offer rotating 24-hour emergency services. Veterinarians should always be willing to confer with their colleagues or specialists to find the best care options for your dog.

Are the hospital's hours convenient, and is the facility located nearby? Many times, veterinary hospitals offer drop-off services in the morning before you go to work. The closer the clinic, the more apt you will be to seek necessary care promptly rather than putting it off for several days until it's more convenient to travel a long distance.

Is the cost something you can manage? Specialty practices typically cost a bit more than general practice care. Of course, when it comes to your dog's health, cheaper isn't necessarily better. The expertise of the veterinarian and staff should come first.

Do you like the veterinarian—does s/he like you? Trust is a huge issue, and you must feel comfortable with the person responsible for your pet's care. The veterinarian you choose should be willing to answer your questions in an understandable fashion, without jargon, and without making you feel "funny" for asking. After all, you both want the best for your pet.

A Partnership For Dog Health

The veterinarian is your partner in health care for the lifetime of your dog. In the best of situations, the veterinarian sees Rex only a couple of times a year.

Meanwhile, you live with him, and that means you know your canine buddy better than anybody. You are in the best position to sound the alarm if your pet feels under the weather, and get him to the veterinarian for the proper care. That's a dynamic and effective health care partnership.

Since you live with your dog and know him the best of all, it's up to you to learn what is "normal" behavior and appearance. That way, you'll easily recognize something that's out of the ordinary, so you can get timely help from your veterinarian.

The veterinarian relies on your information about your pet to provide the best care possible. Does he eat well? Play with enthusiasm? Use the potty regularly, or have intermittent diarrhea where he misses the mark?

Perhaps he favors a leg, or wheezes and coughs after a game of Frisbee-fetch. Or maybe Cinder is the healthiest, best-behaved and prime example of dogdom ever to grace the examining room.

When you take your dog for his veterinary visit, be prepared to answer questions, offer information, and even ask pointed questions of your own. Don't wait to get home to wonder what the doctor meant by something she said—there are *no* stupid questions when it comes to caring for your special dog.

If your dog suffers from fear, ask your veterinarian about pre-exam medical options. There may be prescriptions available that help Cinder better cope with the anxiety, and you may be able to administer this ahead of vet visits—and prevent a lot of doggy angst. Be sure to get all the information you need to make informed decisions about, and properly care for your canine companion.

FOILING FEAR:

AFTER THE VET VISIT

One of the most upsetting forms of interdog aggression occurs between dogs that formerly were best friends. This type of squabble can be emotionally upsetting to the victim dog as well as the pets' owners. In some instances, the unexpected attack results from redirected aggression when the aggressor lashes out at a surrogate target since the actual target can't be reached.

A common scenario occurs when one dog from the household leaves home to go to the groomer or veterinarian. When the dog returns home, former canine or kitty friends either snub the returning dog, get bristly with raised hackles or outright attack the treated dog. It almost appears that the pets don't recognize each other.

Actually, they don't.

Scent Communication Rules

Dogs communicate with vocal, visual and scent cues, and the dog's unique scent serves as the ultimate poochy name tag. When they sleep together, or simply rub against one another in passing, they share scent. Cats may lick-groom their dog friends, too, and this communal shared scent is even more important with cats. It's like a color-coded system that identifies them as belonging to the same family.

When your dog visits the veterinarian, he smells weird upon his return. He's been handled by strangers, perhaps bathed or treated with medicines that smell funny, and may even be ill and smell unhealthy. If he's been anesthetized or sedated, his gait and stance may be altered. He's wearing a foreign smelly name tag the other pets don't readily recognize, so the hackles go up when this "imposter" shows up. The other pets become so leery, they may not be willing to get close enough to establish his true sniff-identity.

When the household pets greet the returning dog with growls or hisses, he naturally gets his back up and acts defensive, too. This situation can escalate beyond the posturing, particularly if the ill dog continues to make trips to and from the vet clinic.

Stop After-Vet-Visit Dog Bashing

Confident dogs usually work out their differences in time. But you can speed up the process, and prevent worsening relationships with these tips.

Try to schedule routine vet visits for your pets at the same time. That way, they all smell similar after being handled by clinic staff. In fact, having a calm, confident dog along with a fearful dog may help reduce the angst. You will need an extra human along to be sure all your dogs are properly supervised.

When a dog is ill, his body chemistry can make him smell funny and other dogs often change their behavior toward him even before the vet visit. Segregate a sick dog from the others, especially if they're treating him poorly. Dog bashing just raises the stress levels of all involved, and the longer it goes on, the more time it will take to reverse.

Segregate the dog returning from the vet in a room alone for at least half a day. Some dogs require a full day of alone-time to recover completely from anesthesia, and to decompress from the vet visit so he's less defensive.

All the pets may be more willing to become reacquainted after a cooling off period. Reintroductions in the yard, where they have room to run and not feel trapped, can also help. Don't rush to re-integrate the your dog to the rest of the family. He may need extra time to get over the vet visit. There's no urgent need to thrust him back with the rest right away.

A cat that returns from the vet often self-grooms and gets rid of the icky clinic and stranger smell within a short time. Dogs don't have that advantage, though, so you can help with some grooming tricks.

A full bath may not be an option, but a dry shampoo or just wiping him down with a damp cloth can help. Then pet your dog from head to toe, or even give him a massage if he enjoys that. This puts YOUR familiar, calming scent back onto your dog.

If your dog's housemates include cat buddies, use a hand towel to pet-pet-pet the other household cats. Pay particular attention to the best-friend cat, rubbing the towel against his cheeks. This gathers the best-friend cat's signature scent, which can then be rubbed over the vet-visit dog to help re-establish communal family scent.

Monitor the first several hours of the pets' interaction. Segregate the treated dog immediately should there be a dog-bashing incident.

THANK YOU FOR READING!

Dear Reader,

I began writing about pets more than twenty years ago—in dog years I should be dead! I hope you enjoyed reading **MY DOG HATES MY VET!** and that it's helped reduce your canine family's fears.

For dog-to-dog angst and a whole lot more canine behavior tips and tricks, find detailed how-to answers in the full-length book, **COMPETABILITY: SOLVING BEHAVIOR PROBLEMS IN YOUR MULTI-DOG HOUSEHOLD.**

Many times I hear from readers who share stories about their dogs and cats, and I'd love to hear from you. Maybe YOUR pet's heartwarming story could be published [on my blog at AmyShojai.com](#) or even included in a future book. All pets deserve to be famous!

I'd like to ask a big favor—could you please post a review of this book (loved it, hated it) as I'd enjoy your feedback. You may not realize how much influence readers like you have to make or break a book simply by sharing your thoughts in a review.

Thank you so much for spending your time with me. Now…go pet your pets!

BIO: Amy Shojai, CABC is Fear Free Certified and an IAABC certified animal behavior consultant and a nationally known authority on pet care. She is the award-winning author of more than 35 cat and dog books and thousands of articles and columns. She served as the Puppies Expert at Puppies.About.com, and the behavior expert at Cats.About.com, and regularly appears on national radio and television including Animal Planet DOGS 101 and CATS 101.

Amy addresses a wide range of fun-to-serious issues in her work, covering training, behavior, health care, and medical topics. She also writes the September Day "Thrillers With Bite" dog viewpoint series featuring a trained Maine Coon cat and German Shepherd service dog.

She and her husband live with assorted critters in North Texas. Amy can be reached at her website at www.shojai.com where you can subscribe to her PETS PEEVES Newsletter and Ask Amy YouTube Channel, like her on Facebook.com/amyshojai.cabc, follow on Twitter @amyshojai, and check out her Bling, Bitches & Blood Blog at AmyShojai.com.

www.ingramcontent.com/pod-product-compliance
Lightning Source LLC
Chambersburg PA
CBHW071727020426
42333CB00017B/2431